Piano • Vocal •

Best of ROBERT

© Michael Putland/RETNAUK

ISBN 978-1-61780-346-8

HAL•LEONARD®
CORPORATION

7777 W. BLUEMOUND RD. P.O. BOX 13819 MILWAUKEE, WI 53213

Visit Hal Leonard Online at
www.halleonard.com

ALL THE KING'S HORSES

Words and Music by ROBERT PLANT,
CLIVE DEAMER, JOHN BAGGOTT,
JUSTIN ADAMS and LIAM TYSON

Folky, with energy

(1.) Swift and true straight to my heart,
(2.) I'm on the out - side look - ing in,
(3.) Guitar solo

love has come call - ing
o - ver and o - ver

and I'm back there a - gain.
and o - ver a - gain.

I pour my - self _ a brand - new start, _
There's no tell - ing where _ I've been, _

glad to _ be fall - ing
how I _ re - turned, _

for the beau - ty with - in. _
how much I have seen. _

Solo ends

(1.,2.) All _____
(3.) Oh. _____

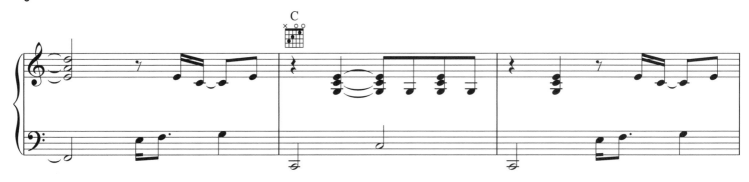

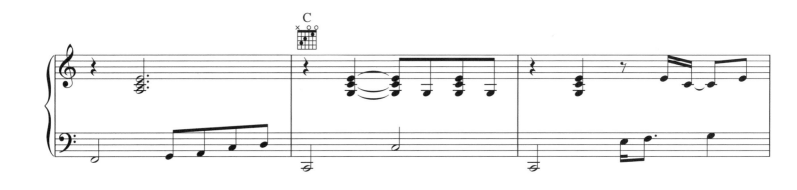

Mmm,

ANGEL DANCE

Written by DAVID HIDALGO
and LOUIS PEREZ

shout   when you hear   them   fall. _____   Let them

fly   right a - cross   the   wall, _____   let them

cry   'til the morn - ing   call. _____   Ah.   Lit - tle an - gel dance. _

Lit - tle an - gel dance. _

BURNING DOWN ONE SIDE

Words and Music by ROBERT BLUNT,
ROBERT PLANT and JEZZ WOODROFFE

Fire down Bou - le - vard d' - A - mour, ___ shoot through the

BIG LOG

Words and Music by ROBERT BLUNT,
ROBERT PLANT and JEZZ WOODROFFE

Mellow Rock

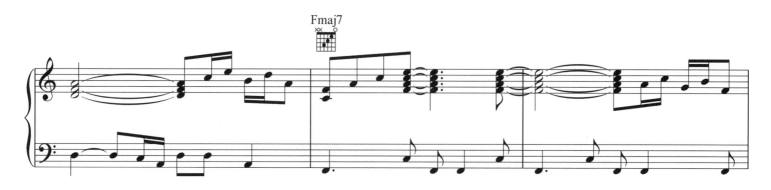

My love is in league _____ with the
My love is miles _____ in the
My love is ex - ceed - ing the
Your love is cra - dled _____ in _____

free - way,   its _____ pas - sion _____ will ride _____ as the
wait - ing,   the _____ eyes that _____ just stare _____ and the
lim - it,   red - eyed _____ and fe - vered with the
know - ing,   eyes in _____ the mir - ror,   still ex -

To Coda ⊕

D.S. al Coda

CODA

jour - ney is done, ___ there is no turn - ing back, ___ no, ___

My love＿ is in league＿ with the free-way,

oh,＿ with the free-way and the com-ing of the

HEAVEN KNOWS

Words and Music by PHILIP JOHNSTONE
and DAVID BARRATT

Additional Lyrics

2. Now I find myself fully occupied and half alive
   With your head, heart, arms and legs wrapped around my family pride.
   See the whites of their eyes, then shoot
   With all the romance of the Ton Ton Macoute.
   Chorus

HURTING KIND
(I've Got My Eyes on You)

Words and Music by ROBERT PLANT,
PHILIP JOHNSTONE, CHRIS BLACKWELL,
DOUG BOYLE and CHARLIE JONES

Driving Rock

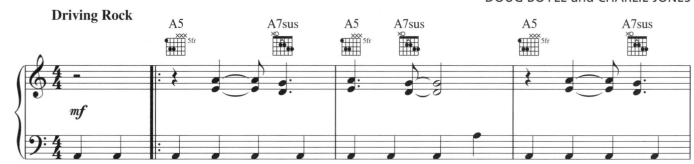

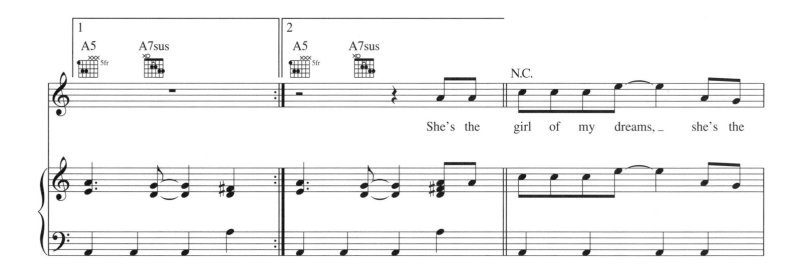

She's the girl of my dreams, _ she's the girl on my mind. _ She used to play me for a fool 'cause she's the hurt-ing kind. _

D.S. al Coda

CODA A5

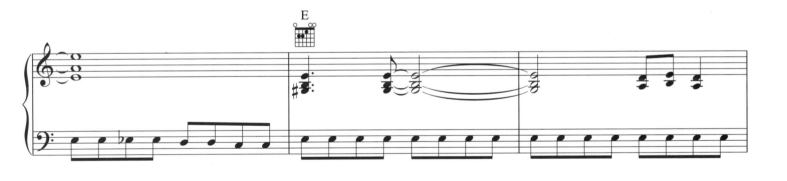

Oh, ___   oh, ___   let's talk a - bout it.

E

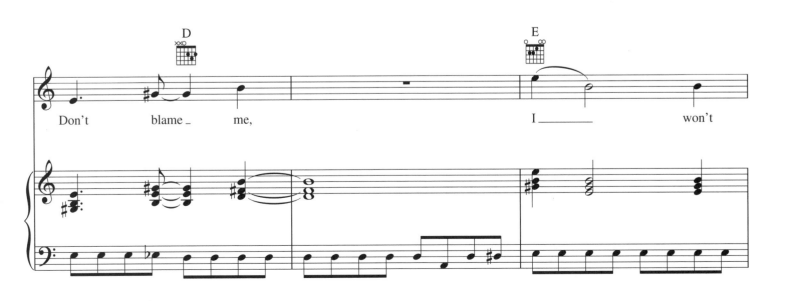

D   E

Don't   blame _ me,   I _____ won't

IN THE MOOD

Words and Music by ROBERT PLANT,
ROBERT BLUNT and PAUL MARTINEZ

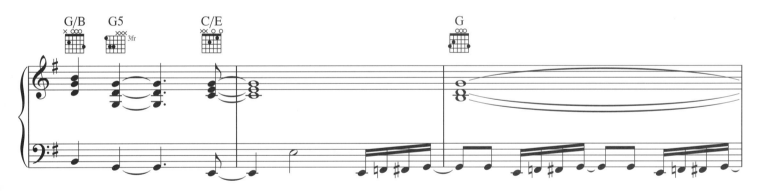

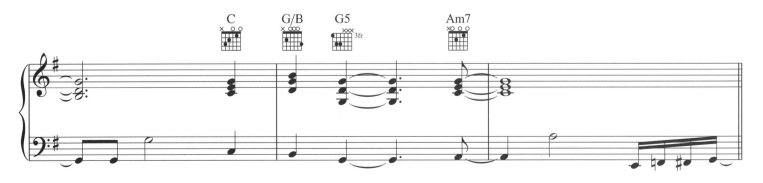

I'm in the mood_ for a mel-o-dy, I'm in the mood_ for a mel-o-dy, I'm in the mood.___
I can make you dance, I can make you sing, I can make you dance, I can make you sing if you want me to.___
An-y lit-tle song that you want to sing,___ lit-tle song that you want to sing, an-y song will do.___

I'm in the mood_ for a mel-o-dy, I'm in the mood_ for a mel-o-dy, I'm in the mood.___
I can make you dance, I can make you sing, I can make you dance, I can make you sing if you want me to.___
An-y lit-tle song that you want to sing,___ lit-tle song that you want to sing, it's up to you.___

I'm in the mood_ for a mel‑o‑dy, I'm in the mood_ for a mel‑o‑dy, I'm in the mood._____
I can make you dance, I can make you sing, I can make you dance, I can make you sing if you want me to._____
An‑y lit‑tle song that you want to sing,___ lit‑tle song that you want to sing, you're_ blue._____

I BELIEVE

Words and Music by ROBERT PLANT
and PHILIP JOHNSTONE

Tears, tears at the wa-
Big fire ___ on top

-ter's edge,
of the hill,

hey, lit-tle sis-ter, give us
a hope-less ges-ture and a

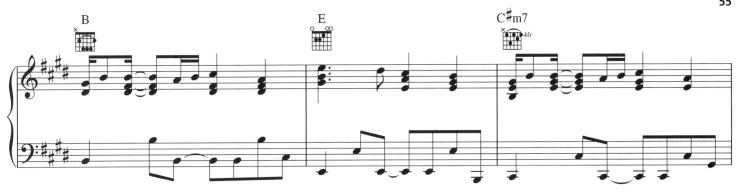

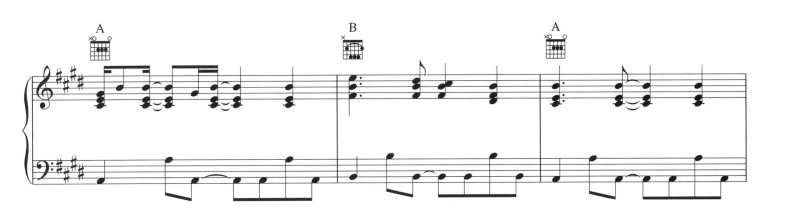

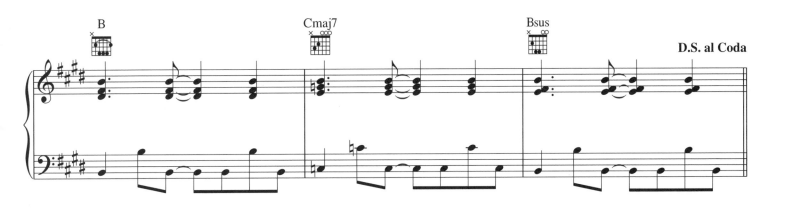

LITTLE BY LITTLE

Words and Music by ROBERT PLANT
and JEZZ WOODROFFE

Rock, with a moderate groove

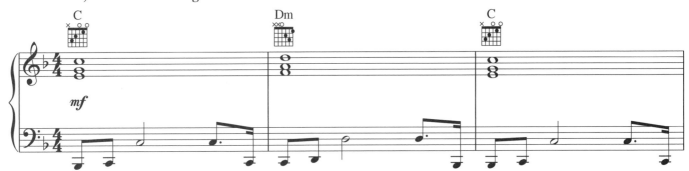

I can breathe a - gain, oh.

Vocal ad lib. on repeat

Call your name, call your name.

Call your name, call your name.

RICH WOMAN

Words and Music by DOROTHY LaBOSTRIE
and McKINLEY MILLET

She got the mon - ey and___ I got the hon - ey.
I know my ba - by and___ she's all mine.___

R.H. tacet 1st time - - - - - - - - - - - - - - -

Called my ba - by late___ last night.___
She give me a Cad - il - lac, a dia - mond ring.___

R.H. tacet 1st time -

She told me, "Dad - dy," ev - 'ry -
She told me, "Dad - dy, don't you

R.H. tacet 1st time -

thing was al - right. ⎱
wor - ry 'bout a thing." ⎰

R.H. tacet 1st time -

She got the mon-ey and __ I got the hon - ey. She got the mon-ey and __

I got the hon - ey. She got the mon-ey and __ I got the hon - ey. __

She's all mine __ and __ I'm so glad. _____

She's the best wom-an that I ev-er had.

She's all mine __ and __ I'm so glad. __ She's all mine __ and __

I'm so glad. __ She's all mine __ and __ I'm so glad. __

Repeat ad lib. and Fade

Vocal ad lib.

PLEASE READ THE LETTER

Words and Music by ROBERT PLANT,
JIMMY PAGE, MICHAEL PEARSON
and STEPHEN JONES

Violin

D.S. al Coda

CODA

Please read the let-ter, I nailed it to your door._ It's

Repeat ad lib. and Fade

TALL COOL ONE

Words and Music by ROBERT PLANT
and PHILIP JOHNSTONE

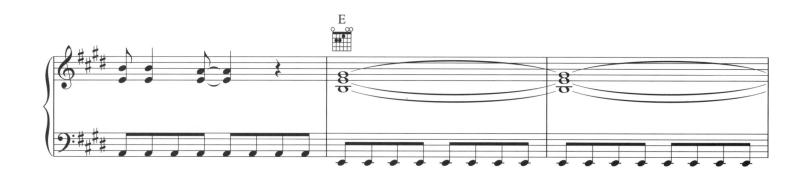

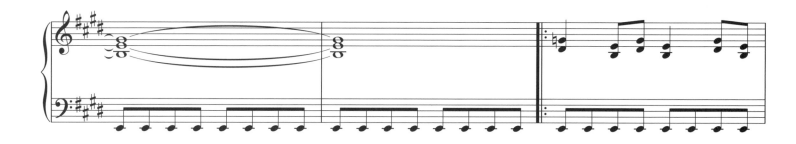

TIE DYE ON THE HIGHWAY

Words and Music by ROBERT PLANT
and CHRISTOPHER BLACKWELL

Driving Rock

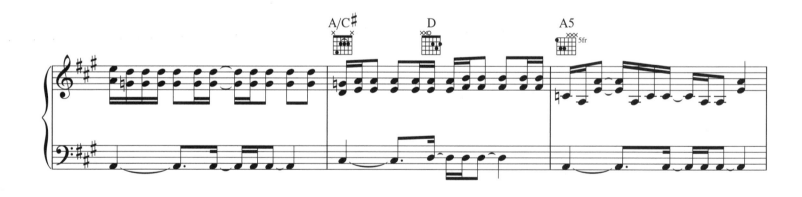

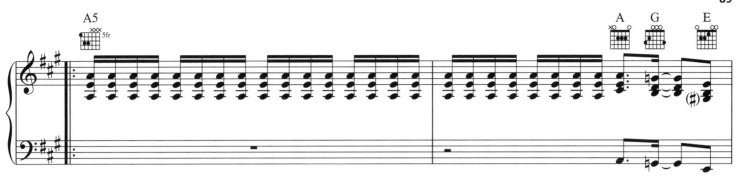

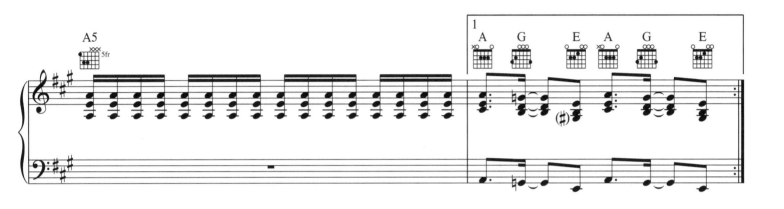

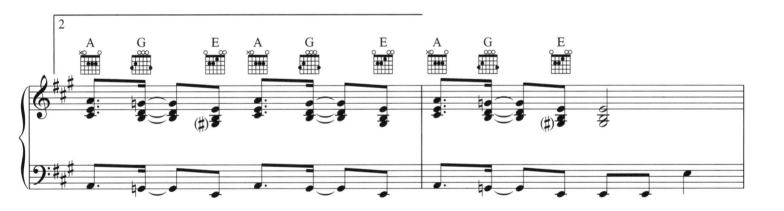

D.S. al Coda

We must _ be in heav- en, yeah?

29 PALMS

Words and Music by ROBERT PLANT,
PHILIP JOHNSTONE, DOUG BOYLE
and CHARLIE JONES

Ba - by, now. _____ It comes kind of hard ___ when I

hear your voice_ on the ra - di - o. Lead-ing me back_ down the road _

D Em G C
that leads back to you. Oh, don't you hear me, ba - by, now.
G D G
Twen - ty - nine Palms, I feel the heat of your des -
C G
ert heart. Lead - ing me back down the road
D Em G
that leads back to you, you,

SHIP OF FOOLS

Words and Music by ROBERT PLANT
and PHILIP JOHNSTONE

Moderately slow Rock

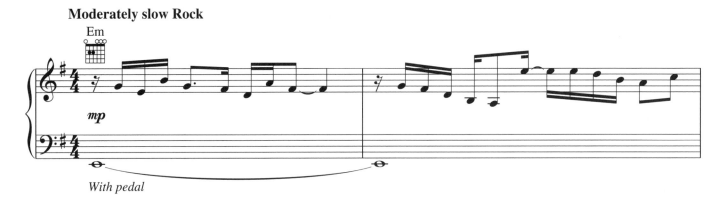

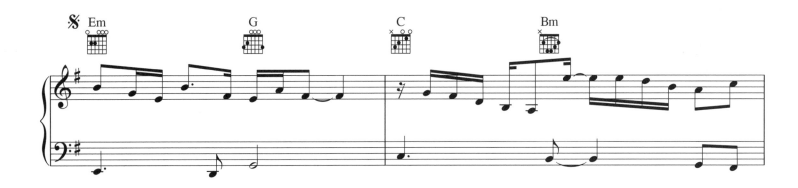

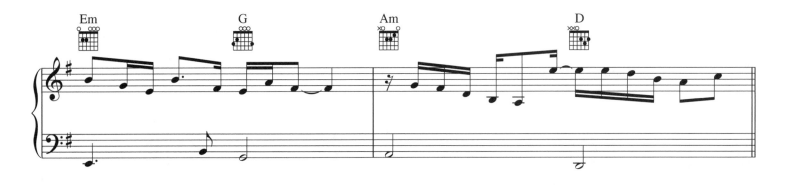

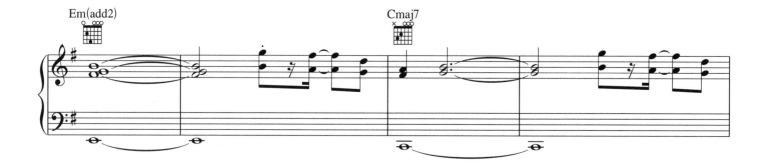

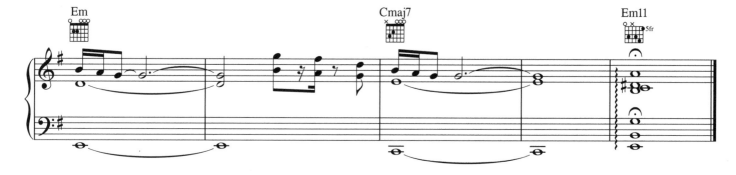

Additional Lyrics

2. Beneath a lover's moon I'm waiting.
   I am the pilot of the storm,
   Adrift in pleasure I may drown.
   I built this ship; it is my making.
   And, furthermore, my self control,
   I can't rely on anymore.
   I know why, I know why.
   Chorus

3. You claim that no man is an island
   While I land up in jeopardy
   More distant from you by degrees.
   I walk this shore in isolation
   And at my feet eternity
   Draws ever sweeter plans for me.
   I know why, I know why.
   Chorus